MORGAN SILAS DONNELLY

ECHOES
OF THE DEEP

Enchanted Beginnings of
Love, Renewal, and Awakening

Flotsam and Jetsam Series
Book 1

Copyright © 2024 by Morgan Silas Donnelly.

All rights reserved. No part of this book may be reproduced or used in any manner without written permission of the copyright owner except for the use of quotations in a book review. For more information, contact: writer@morgansilasdonnelly.com.

ISBN Paperback: 978-1-7382574-3-0
ISBN Electronic: 978-1-7382574-4-7

Publishing Consultant: PRESStinely - PRESStinely.com

This book is a work of fiction. The names, characters, and events in this book are the products of the author's imagination or are used fictitiously. Any similarity to real persons, living or dead, is coincidental and not intended by the author.

Printed in the United States of America.

Morgan Silas Donnelly
Tiny Gnat Publishing

tiny gnat
publishing

MorganSilasDonnelly.com

Dedication

To those who loved … and found something magnificent.

And to my muse.

Table of Contents

Foreword 11

Preface 15

Love
and roses and sunflowers

What Would Love Do? 18
Stolen Kisses 20
Stolen Kisses
    redux 21
What Would Love Do?
    alternate 22
Vagrant's Lament
    dedicated to all the nomads 24
The Good Lady 25
Woke 26
The Whisper 27
Beauty 28
Collision 29
Her Song 30
Lips of Gold, Skin of Honey 31
Fine 32
Not Needed On Voyage 33
You Close Your Eyes 34
Inside 35
Words Are 36
It Was A Very Sweet Start 37
You 38

Regal Pair 39
Regal Pair
    coda 40
Remember When? 41
The Row Boat 42
Playlists 43
The Twirl 44
Sounds Pathetic 45
Sounds Pathetic
    rawr edition 46
Last Kiss Goodnight 47
Goodnight Kiss Last 48

Connections
and celebrations and regrets

Birthday Card 50
Lost Boy ... Found 51
Blank Birthday Card 52
You Know (The Know) 53
Blank Birthday Card
    redux 54
Blank Birthday Card
    remixed 56
Where Do You Wander? 58
Maybe 59
Look! There!! 60
Magical Moments 61
The Mouse 62
Best of Me 64
Circles 65
Grow Up Kid! 66
Their Love 67

Life
and laughter and fire

Oh, Do I Need To Stay Silent?.. 70
Be..73
I AM
    where the wild things are..74
Laughter Incarnate 75
Jasmine Tea + Flowers 76
Pleading..77
Cog.. 78
Celebrations...79
Adrift.. 80
Wet Coast Campfire...81
Tribe Hate..82
Playtime... 83
Playtime
    alternate version 84
Playtime Over 85
Playground..86
Shame Yard Of Lies 87
Prayer Time 88
Context
    original flavour 89
Context
    with added Vitamin C..90
Unfolding..91
I'm Starting To Understand...92
Machine Gun It... 93
I Asked
    original mix 94
I Asked
    dot calm mix 95

3 Vees	96
Terrors	97
Mirror Me	98
Run Away	99
Run Away alternative beat	100
When The Power Goes Out	101
I Was Thinking About My Life	102
Ho Hum	104
Eventually	105
Happy	106
Raging	107
Throw Away	108
2022 A.D.	109
Shalt	110
Game It Up!	111
The Devil's Due	112

Prose
and farming implements and cooking accoutrements, oh my

Angel	114
A Pitchfork, A Blanket And A 6 Pack	116
... I Was Asked ...	119
Snowing Here Late December 2021	121
Goom-Bye 2021!	123
The Coat	126
Tears	128
Remember The Oven Mitt	130
Cloud Girl	132
Man At War	134
Sludge Attack	136

Table of Contents

No Mercy 138
Storm Front 139
To My Friends 141

The Series **143**

Meet Morgan **145**

A Note To The Reader **147**

Foreword

As a professional in the integrative healing world, I work mostly with how the physical body responds to emotional, mental, and spiritual experiences, healthy or not. Within my practice, as well as within my own life, I witness the immense love as well as pain that comes with true love and heartbreak. It can be confusing and debilitating, often stopping many in their tracks for years and looping themselves into patterns of choosing unavailable people as they subconsciously wait for their love to return. What I have noticed is a lack of understanding of love and how it shapes our lives, how it changes us to become better versions of who we are, and how it unlocks certain codes of growth and expansion.

This is why I was so honoured by my dear friend, Morgan Donnelly when he asked me to read some of the poetry he has laid out for this wonderful book *Echoes of the Deep*.

I have known Morgan for many years. We met through connections in a different city I used to live in, and we quickly bonded through a shared passion and love for healing and growth.

I was always taken aback by Morgan's use of metaphors, attention to detail, and the creativity with which he can relate a story to a unique life experience. I truly consider him to be one of the deepest wordsmiths I have ever encountered. You can be assured in any of Morgan's writings that he will have enchanted the words throughout, your eyes eagerly taking in each word as it paints a visual so clear it is like watching a movie in your mind.

He will take you through the highs and lows of the fullest emotional expression, so be ready to laugh, cry, and reminisce as he takes you through a deep, profound life experience and initiation.

When I first began to read his poems, we were sitting down at a beautiful coffee shop, sipping on lattes, laughing about the craziness of life and how you can experience such deep, profound love. His smile as he brought out the manuscript, gently laying his heart on paper into my hands, made me know I was in for something special.

I began to smile wide, leaning into his honest experience, feeling his excitement as the rollercoaster of this experience began its ascent, taking me through joy and eagerness. His powerful words created butterflies as my eyes danced on each word, hungrily moving from one to the next. As I turned each page, I savoured each poetic rhythm and symbolism, feeling the high as I noticed the poems begin to start their slow descent.

As the mood changed, I could feel a storm brewing inside my stomach. I felt the aching and longing, the grief, and I noticed tears beginning to well in my eyes. I could not get enough. I sat quietly, going through the full spectrum of emotions as he sat contently, sipping on his coffee. He said, "You know you don't have to read it all right now!" with his signature giggle, but once you start, you just cannot stop!

Foreword

He has a way of hooking you into each word, taking you down a river of experiences between the calm, the chaos, the serenity. I lost track of time, as I always do, regardless of whether he was speaking or I'm reading something he had created. His ability to evoke emotions while being so relatable in an experience most of us have had - real, deep love and heartbreak. His creative gift initiated a large healing response within me as I recounted a deep love that had gotten away in my life. Memories I had forgotten surfaced. The tenderness, gentleness, and groundedness of his masculine energy were exactly what I needed to soften and peer into the depths of my own soul, what I was holding onto without realising it until I saw his truest expression of love. This is a mark of a true master of their craft, the ability to take you through your own experience through the lens of their experience. To create such a safe place within your own mind that you can go deeper into your perception of your life through his work.

It isn't just Morgan's experience; it is an experience so many of us can relate to one another. He makes it not only fun but introspective.

If you had told me that poetry could make me feel so many emotions and have so many memories at once, I would have said, "Try me." Well, Morgan has and did. He activated me in such a way that not only did I have so many synchronicities after the fact, but it also got my creative juices flowing!

So if you're ready to experience the magic that is Morgan, trust me, you will never be disappointed. You will stay captivated, longing for more, and believe me, he will deliver.

I am so grateful for his work and his continued friendship. Dear reader, I know that you will love this book for all of the reasons above. You will never be poetically edged and let down or disappointed. He will have you reading over and over and over again, rediscovering your love of poetry and a well-written story. Thank you again, Morgan, for your presence, your creativity, your friendship, and your deep sense of compassion and empathy. You are truly a Divine Man, and I am so grateful to have you in my life. To all the readers, enjoy every moment. I know you will truly feel the depth of his articulation.

Cassandra Finch
Founder of Phoenix School of Alignment
www.phoenixschoolofalignment.com

Preface

There are many words in this book. Their genesis was Love. A love that opened my creativity and heart in ways I had no way of predicting when that door was flung wide open. Some days I still pinch myself to see if this life is real.

The written words that follow, with their layered meanings, are a construct to bring to me, and to you, a splinter of the majesty of what I experienced in the years encompassing 2018-2022.

The construct of the poems, ponderings, and prose as I write them is a thing of organized chaos, a way of making sense of a world that no longer makes sense after what I experienced and yet, in the same breath, makes complete sense to my widening vision.

Nothing pleases me more than to twist and prod the English language into word art as a way of expressing feelings or conveying peculiar scenery. Occasionally, I swear or incorporate grammatical errors or just plain mince words beyond recognition to bring chaos to the organized.

#longlivewordart

Morgan Silas Donnelly
June 2024

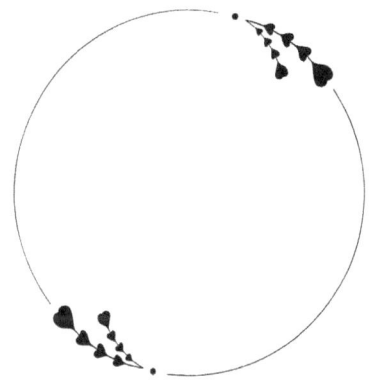

Love

and roses and sunflowers

What Would Love Do?

A moonlit walk
on crunching snow
past sentinel trees
Biscotti and lattes in a crowded cafe
two hearts glowing in small talk
That's what Love would do

Old woman kneels by her man
hand in hand they lived one life
Now she lives on
Today a fresh rose lays on his stone
so he knows he will never be alone
That's what Love would do

Drums beat faster, war is near
Rage of hate
weapons to sear
The pyres of madness infect a nation
while the world prays for growing anger's ablation
That's what Love would do

You never wrote me a poem
using pen and paper
You sing from the heart
a melody to croon
A sweet, sweet melody of
hope, longing and desire
Now every morning when I rise
I can hum the tune
That's what Love would do

~ Love ~

With a fire that
transforms
consumes
transcends
but does not burn
As the World cries out to learn
what Love can do

Stolen Kisses

"I stole that kiss" I declared.

"Yes, good sire, you did."

"It was only so that in a time and a place of your choosing, you would know it was perfectly appropriate to kiss me back. Not as chattel, not as the duty of one to another, but as a sovereign soul enrapturing another sovereign soul in a moment of the deepest love and connection." I stated.

I continued "If you feel to kiss me, kiss me like that."

~ Love ~

Stolen Kisses
redux

I once stole a kiss from you.

It was to let you know it was safe to kiss me back ... when you decided to.

What Would Love Do?
alternate

A moonlit walk
on crunching snow
past sentinel trees
Biscotti and cortados in a crowded cafe
two hearts glowing in small talk
That's what Love would do

Old man walking with his wife
oh so slow
Hand in hand they live one life
By the lake, she skips a stone
He hands her a rose
so she knows she will never be alone
That's what Love would do

Drums beat faster, war is near
Rage of hate
weapons to sear
The pyres of madness infect a nation
while the world prays for glowing anger's abation
That's what Love would do

So alone I seem in the day
yet while I slumber
a sweet melody my lover croons
Upon my head moonbeams play
while my love bares their soul to the moon
A haunting song of dreams and longing

~ Love ~

and in the morning I hum that tune
That's what Love would do

With a fire that
transforms
consumes
transcends
but does not burn
As the World cries out to learn
what Love can do

Vagrant's Lament
dedicated to all the nomads

In a window sill picture frame
golden clouds swim in turquoise skies
While this nomad feels no shame
in witnessing the age old game

You wait for me in a desert brown
One day soon I will again be around
for eyes that twinkle and
flirt with a wink
My heart was battered
My heart was bruised
Kiss by kiss it shall not sink

My lover has electric touch
that even now is more than memory
Which to this vagrant's soul means so much
as I stare with a pillow to clutch

~ Love ~

The Good Lady

The Good Lady over yonder
will sometimes let her heart wander

Gather courage boys and tap the cask
you'll need heart and soul for this task

With a smile, she can shed her clothes
but to part with her armour
she is loathe

When asked for simple things
she can fidget
The chasm is deep but oh, the king's
ransom if you can bridge it

The cups are dry
The songs are sung
The friends go off one by one
On the wall your keys are hung

Familiar home and hearth
dark and dreary seem
Have faith, good Sir
there is no armour while we dream

Woke

I woke this morning
to a dream, still fresh
You had curled up in the night
and placed your head on my stomach

    You make life worth living

~ Love ~

The Whisper

I whispered to you last night in your dreams

It wasn't pleading
It wasn't whining
It wasn't cursing
It was heartfelt longing for a lover missing

Perhaps you heard it as a whisper
Perhaps you heard it as a shout
Mayhap you heard it as a breeze rustling
the willow weeping
as the brook gave comfort in burbling song

My arms are empty
My heart is broken
Come sit at my table
there is a place set just for you

Beauty

The beauty of the experience far outweighs the potential for heartbreak.

~ Love ~

Collision

Our worlds are different
and yet the same at fundamental zones

When our worlds collide, there are sparks
<< echos in metallic tones >>

Truth be told, there is

                                              no
        I would rather collide with
                                              one

Her Song

It's 22:22 and my baby ain't here
She's somewhere down south
and I can't reach her there

Sugar + spice + everything nice
She's the beat that makes
my heart thump true
I think of her and then
I can never be blue

Our two lives have twined into one
She's the girl who has my
heart and soul
The moon and stars shine so bright
There ain't no reason on Earth
we will ever be undone

Barefoot in the park chasing after larks
Our feet up on the dock, fishing poles in hand
Waiting for a bite, feels so right

Her Irish eyes look in mine
my soul is bared ain't no denials
When my baby smiles + the stars align
I know there will be an end to my trials

~ Love ~

Lips of Gold, Skin of Honey

Your photo is on my phone
Your electricity is on my skin
Your wine is on my lips

Fine

I used to think
    the quality was in the quantity

    until I found
the quantity in the quality

~ Love ~

Not Needed On Voyage

I no longer need protection around my heart.

For sale: used bricks. Cheap.

You Close Your Eyes

We meet. We smile. We talk.
We laugh. We trade little secrets
in a sly kind of way, whispers between someones new.
I ask to kiss you.
You nod and wet your lips.
You close your eyes.

We walk. We skip along hand in hand.
Our time slips away. The clock unwinds
in a fun kind of way, moments oozing between someones familiar.
I catch the eyes of another.
You turn your head and flip your hair.
You close your eyes.

We dance.
We drink. We sing.
We fuck.
The sweet pleasure
in a delightful kind of way, builds between someones comfortable.
You close your eyes and say the name of another.
I close my eyes.

~ Love ~

Inside

When I was empty inside
    I feared losing you
    I fear losing you
Now that I am full inside

Words Are

Words are important to me.
I suppose that is why they sting

      when used in anger.

~ Love ~

It Was A Very Sweet Start

I feared rebuttal
as this child will play
So the last text was subtle
my topsy turvy affirmation started with a "K"

Now here is the deep dark night
but my candle burns bright
and my only desire
is to stoke the fire

You

Snow has stopped falling
on my cold, cold land
The world is dark, quiet and still
The air is alive, waiting for spring
to burst forth again

The fire is stoked, the candles lit just so
The couch placed perfectly
fluffy pillows and soft blankets
Hot chocolate poured for 2
    - whip cream if it pleases -

Your lover is ready
No pressure

    No rush

Anticipation is sweet too my love

~ Love ~

Regal Pair

My finger wears a ring
It is a memory of a thing
gold, perfect and round
of a time when love was unbound

I swept
       and I mopped
             the dirt
                     from my heart

It helped me forget that we are

       now apart

I was so proud and distracted that, yes,
I did miss a spot
       my lover is gone

       I cry a lot

I had my reunion hopes
placed into bottles
and
then overboard tied
to my own private yacht

Across the waves I hear Pandora weep and
into my heart
a coolness seeps...

Regal Pair

coda

The King sits on his throne
His Bride sits beside
The Jester adjusts his fabric crown and dances a jig
The regal pair pay no attention
They are lost in Love and the chatter is pretension

~ Love ~

Remember When?

Remember way back when?
We both said our relationship
was a long shot -- the longest of long shots

I figured out why we said that
We were listening to other people's voices

                        Grumpy
                              Lonely
                                      People
                                                Sad

You know how we made it babe?
Our hearts sang in

                        Joyful
                                Blissful
                                      Harmony
                                            Delightful

We held hands and listened to that song
                        all night long

The Row Boat

Promises kept, promises broken
Love was but a token
Flowers lament
A letter is sent

Jackyl wails, raven screech
Emotions teach
The vine that withers
and a laugh that titters

A cool grey mist
A long slow boat row
in waves that make it list
Love sails away
love will return

                     ... one day

~ Love ~

Playlists

I like myself more, now that I have deleted some playlists.

The Twirl

A broken heart can always mend
When eyes lose focus
time will twirl and bend

Past

Present

Future

~ Love ~

Sounds Pathetic

"So what do you think of that plan forward for us?"

"It sounds passionless and purposeless - very wishy washy. I would rather have a long, intimate talk with you about a myriad of meaningful topics, and then sneak with you to the back of the cafe where we passionately and deeply kiss in a bathroom stall."

I cleared my throat, sipped my drink and continued "But, you know if you are rather just looking for surface stuff, the next contestant will be along soon" as our gazes met full on.

Sounds Pathetic
rawr edition

"So what do you think of that platonic plan for us?"

"It sounds passionless and purposeless - very wishy washy and trivial compared to the feelings I have for you. I would rather sneak you into a graffitied bathroom stall in the back of this bar and ravage you like the sex toy you so, so sumptuously are."

I cleared my throat and continued "But, you know if you are rather just looking for surface stuff, the next contestant will be along soon enough for you after I walk out of here alone" as our gazes met head on.

~ Love ~

Last Kiss Goodnight

If I had known that was the last kiss
                between us
I would have kissed you longer
                and a lot more stronger

Goodnight Kiss Last

If I had known that was the last kiss
between us

and stronger
I would have kissed you longer

Connections

and celebrations and regrets

Birthday Card

I didn't know you at 6
when your dolly needed a stitch
I didn't know you at 13
when your mother was such a bitch

I didn't know you at 17
when the world was yours to take
I didn't know you at 22
when life was yours to make

I didn't know you at 25
when your heart would sink
I didn't know you at 29
when a tattoo you would ink

But I know you now
Nothing I say can take the candles away
and you have never looked more beautiful
than you do today

~ Connections ~

Lost Boy ... Found

I have only ever been a Lost Boy
I am scared of being Found

I am afraid of being rescued and complete

I give myself permission
        to grow ~~pu~~ up
        to make mistakes
        to heal
        to hear all my voices
        to love
        to be unafraid
        to speak my mind
        to live in abundance
        to live each day with
        an open and kind heart

Blank Birthday Card

The cover artwork grabbed me right away

Maybe it was the colours
Maybe it was the way Mother Nature
sang to
      Her

Maybe it was her pose
Confident
Commanding
      Beautiful

Birthdays don't mean much to me
they are meaningless numbers
I am much more interested in memories
and I
      Love

all the ones we have made so far!

~ Connections ~

You Know (The Know)

You know how we kept finding each other?
We didn't believe
that the other was   to us

        EVER.

             lost

Blank Birthday Card
redux

The cover artwork grabbed me right away
It was her familiar pose
Confident
Commanding
Beautiful

It was the way Mother Nature
sang to her of glory
                     |

vibrated along with the colours
                Bright
                Bold
                Mesmerizing

Birthdays don't mean much to me
they are meaningless numbers
I am much more interested in memories
                        And
I love all the ones we have made so far!

May your day, may your very soul
be filled with
                Exuberance
                Rapture
                Peace

~ Connections ~

This is for

                              You

on your very special day!

Blank Birthday Card
remixed

The cover artwork grabbed me right away
It was her familiar pose
Confident
Commanding
Beautiful

It was the way Mother Nature
sang to her of colourful glory
Bright
Bold
Mesmerizing

Birthdays don't mean much to me
they are meaningless numbers
on the cosmic scorecard

                        I

am much more interested in memories
and bonds and
                        Love

all the ones we have made so far!

May your day, may your very soul
be filled with
Exuberance
Rapture

~ Connections ~

Peace

This is for
                                         You

on your very special day!

Where Do You Wander?

"Where do you wander?" she asked.

"Where the magic is!" he replied.

"Take me there!" she pleaded.

"No." was all he said.

"Oh! Sorry!" she muttered as she turned to leave.

"I can not take you there, but you are welcome to meet me there." he affirmed boldly to the back of her head.

Smiling, the two walked hand in hand to magicland.

~ Connections ~

Maybe

Maybe they got together for lust.

Maybe they were drunk.

Maybe they were lonely.

Maybe he had a nice car.

Maybe she had a new boob job and the confidence to wear it well.

Maybe they wanted to start a family.

Maybe two sparks reached out in recognition of the other and declared without shame

"Baby, let's ignite this world!"

Look! There!!

On a windswept precipice
golden sun warms her chrysalis

S-l-o-w-l-y

M-e-t-h-o-d-i-c-a-l-y

The prism breaks
for all the world to see
This woman in full bloom

The rock hides no more
this woman in full bloom
Birth Death Hate Love Sky + Stars
All will know their doom
for she is a woman in full bloom

In love her heart shatters
and a thousand pieces scatter
into warm fertile ground
waiting for snowfall's sound

In the moment of antithesis
Look! There!!
A chrysalis

~ Connections ~

Magical Moments

Do you know how I know
there is magic in the world?

    I have felt your smile

The Mouse

There once was a mouse
Who locked herself in a cage
for there was a kitty you see
who was all in a rage

The cat would growl
The cat would prowl
The mice would scurry and the
hungry cat would howl

Upon spying the mouse in her cage
the cat smiled a Cheshire grin
"Why my sweet little morsel ... won't you please let me in"

The mouse was polite but declined without fright
for the key you don't see is well out of sight

The cat searched high, the cat searched low
and did find the key to deal
that rodent a death blow

The cage was gilded but the lock was rusty
and our hapless hero got mighty dusty
The cat waited on a lark
through seven days of light and dark

"How now Miss Mouse?
I am hungry and cold
(as you must be)
for you have been in prison long.

~ Connections ~

Come to me! Be bold!!"

"Why no Mr. Cat, not me.
For this trap door you now see
let's me be free! And for all your rage
you have spent 7 days
in an even bigger cage."

Best of Me

I'm not trying to be on my best behaviour.

I'm striving to be the best version of myself when I communicate with you.

~ Connections ~

Circles

Be the completed circle that attracts a completed circle.

Grow Up Kid!

I didn't grow up
because you asked me to.

I didn't grow up
because I was afraid of disappointing you.

I didn't even grow up because I wanted to.

I grew up because you inspired me to.

~ Connections ~

Their Love

Their love was like ice cream

He was pistachio
She was vanilla caramel

He was nuts and she was sweet

Life

and laughter and fire

Oh, Do I Need To Stay Silent?

Oh, do I need to stay silent?
Do I need to comply?
It is safer that way.
Yes, much safer.
Men do not shout at me, women do not shun me.

The mob at night, with their torches bright
do not barge in my door
and steal away my dreams.
Oh to be silent, oh to blend in!
I can hide in plain sight!
I can be free to speak with the pain in my head.

The shadow that knows and the shadow that grows
inside each of them.
I see!
Oh yes, I see!
Don't whisper a thing, there are bad men about.

For the shadow is beside me now, telling me to be still.
Telling me to be a good little child.
Don't whisper a thing, there are bad men about!

I nod my agreement, silent as a mouse.
"Yes. Yes child." Murmurs the shadow.
Another in its grip.

The covers pulled tight, I huddle and shake.
What's that!
Oh, a twinge! A thump!

~ Life ~

"OH MY GOD I have a heart!"

Boom, boom!
"No, no! Be quite quiet heart! The monsters will hear!"
BOOM, BOOM, BOOM!

"AHHHHHHH!"

"NOOOOOO!"

"Heart be quiet! Heart be still!
The mob can hear you, the mob is near!"

BOOM! BOOM! BOOM! BOOM!
"Ok, ok. I'll talk to you. Just be quiet."
Quiet and still, like a good little child.

My heart told me stories.
Beautiful stories.
Stories with butterflies and unicorns playing together in a land with
rivers of chocolate and mountains of ice cream!
Oh so high!
No one was quiet. No one was still!
They all got along by talking aloud!
Oh how strange!
No mobs, no torches, no doors broken down!

Oh my!
My door is shattered, my room is alight!
Oh no!
The mob found me, they heard!

Echoes Of The Deep

As my heart slowly went quiet and still
I heard it say very softly
"The mob is without, the dream is within."

~ Life ~

Be

Be the noise you want to hear in the world.

I AM

where the wild things are

No ropes to bar
no chains to tie
no injury to die
Where the wild things are

A marshmallow for the pyre
a tent and a song for the campfire
They shine so bright, those stars in sky
All is calm
no need to ask why
Where the wild things are

Ferocious claws, burning eyes
all in a package twice your size
                          Be afraid!
                Run away and scream!
        Be brave!
Turn around and see the dream

Where the wild things are

Creature of Terror is your brother
look without eyes and see his mother
Bring Her to Him
Angels will sing hymns

Where the wild things are

~ Life ~

Laughter Incarnate

An elephant parade, a clown handstands
Cotton candy and children's laughter
When the universe expands

Friends and foes, lovers and family
All can be lent
The splinter of purpose, a fragment of life
When the universe is bent

A star. A planet. Behold!
Spinning wheels and rushing energy
When the universe folds

May it never abate
A moment of connection
A moment of tranquility
When the universe is incarnate

Jasmine Tea + Flowers

A cough, a runny nose
housecoat dirty and stained
A life long love brings a dinner plate

A playful pup while
shaky hands raise a chipped cup
Steady hands light the candles for
a long overdue romantic sup

Soft music plays a well worn
melody that never ceases
Chapped lips smack for a taste
of a favourite meal
<< cut into bite size pieces >>

Quick a dab of tissues to
staunch the tears
A knowing nod and 4 eyes say
"Good bye Love"
but only for now

Jasmine tea and flowers spill on the floor

~ Life ~

Pleading

Chattering all day long
there is an idiot on stage
Shattered is the calm
when the idiot
starts a rage

A clear blue sky, a baby's cry
all mean nothing when
you can't even try

A needle, a machine, a bottle
all your actions are just a coddle

A fisherman casts, a policeman cuffs
all you do is cry tough
Begging and pleading
won't do the seeding

A life can be saved and a life can be cherished
If only once more, hope isn't perished

Cog

In the twilight of the old world's dusk
works a man who is but a husk
Gnarled hands, dirty boots
toiling for his master's loot

Honest and simple
this man thinks not of grandeur
and is fearful of missing his
seat at the Father's table

This man is a tool
This man is a cog
This man toils with purpose and beauty
built upon years of steady practice
What some would call a slog
he sees plain as duty

~ Life ~

Celebrations

I don't much believe in birthdays, weddings or funerals. I get the need for connection. I get the need for celebration. I just don't put a lot of onus on the event. The greeting card moments -- five dollars each if you please!

I am the one that is there a week or two later. The one who is there after the circus has left and the leftovers are eaten.

The one who says "how are you friend?" when there is no one else around.

So "how are you friend? Was the celebration amazing? There are only us two here. You have my undivided attention!"

So "how are you friend? Tell me everything. I am all yours."

Adrift

An armada of battle clouds
Adrift on the wind
Float to where the war din is loud

~ Life ~

Wet Coast Campfire

Howling wind, pouring rain
wet wet wet
Presto Log, gasoline, kindling
Burn the green logs
burn burn burn
Oregon Campfire

Tribe Hate

One tribe kicking the ass of another tribe only lasts until their ass is kicked in turn.

~ Life ~

Playtime

Playtime is over.
Some are leaving the sandbox behind.
Some haven't learned how to change their own diapers.

Playtime
alternate version

Playtime is over.
No more hiding your spark of divine love.

~ Life ~

Playtime Over

Want another indication playtime is over??
Your parents take away the toy you've been hitting the other children with.

Playground

The past is a museum
The future is a candy store
The present is a playground

~ Life ~

Shame Yard Of Lies

play ground
shame ground
battle ground
grave yard

Prayer Time

The Single's Dinner Prayer:

"Lord, let me eat this leftover meal from the back of the fridge without getting a tummy ache. Amen."

~ Life ~

Context
original flavour

In our convoluted lives, you ask for content
when the only context that matters
is inside your
heart

Context
with added Vitamin C

In our convoluted lives,
you ask clearly for clarity
in the context of my
content

When the only context that matters
is inside
the content of your own chest
cavity

~ Life ~

unfolding

    It is delicious to savour the
possibilities

probabilities

permutations
    of the unfolding future ahead of us all

I'm Starting To Understand

I'm starting to understand why Gandhi said to turn the other cheek.
I'm starting to understand why Rodney King asked us "can't we all get along?"
I'm starting to understand the terror of a man who said he couldn't breathe.
I'm starting to understand how lepers were shunned.
I'm starting to understand how the world felt in 1918.
I'm starting to understand the children's rhyme "husha husha we all fall down!"
I'm starting to understand why Star Trek is entrenched in pop culture like its contemporaries aren't.
I'm starting to understand who was for the unification of the United Kingdom and who was opposed.
I'm starting to understand why old time clocks tick, then tock, then tick again.
Or is it tock, then tick? I lose myself in the rhythm and I have to start to again....

I'm starting to understand who hid Anne Frank.
I'm starting to understand who turned her in.
I'm starting to understand the change of the seasons.
I'm starting to welcome the change of the seasons.
I'm starting to understand and welcome me.

~ Life ~

Machine Gun It

To the friends who machine gunned me to death in long ago wars, I love you.
To the friends I machine gunned to death in wars long ago, I love you.
To the friends in times of old who's swords ran me through, I love you.
To the friends who I in turn killed with my sword, I love you.
To the friends I saved in ages long ago, with herbs, bandages and poultices, I love you.
To the friends I couldn't save in years past because I no longer had the tools or the knowledge to heal your ills, I love you too.

Please forgive me and stand beside me today. I need a hug.

Desperately.

Maybe you do too.

I Asked

original mix

I asked the wind. I heard whooshing.
I asked the tall grass. I heard rustling.
I asked the river. I heard burbling.
I asked the fire. I heard crackling.

I raged at the Universe "WHY??"

    I got silence.

My heart grew cold.

    I got silent.

and so it went.

One perfectly normal day
I did perfectly normal things.
Laundry.
Dusting.
Shopping.
I prepared meals.
I lived life.

In a silent moment, I understood.
The Universe replies with silence
so we can just be.

~ Life ~

I Asked

dot calm mix

I asked the wind. I heard whooshing.
I asked the tall grass. I heard rustling.
I asked the river. I heard burbling.
I asked the fire. I heard crackling.

I raged at the Universe "WHY??"

I got   silence.

My heart grew cold.

I got   silent.

and so it went

One perfectly normal day
I did perfectly normal things.
Laundry.
Dusting.
Shopping.
I prepared meals.
I lived life.

In a silent moment, I understood.
The Universe replies with

              silence

so we can just be.

3 Vees

    Verses

Versus

    Viruses

Versus

    Verses

~ Life ~

Terrors

Some are peace keepers.
Some are peace makers.
Some are peace upsetters.

Holy terrors are sometimes all three.

Mirror Me

"Hello mirror, my old friend."

"What beauty will you show me today?"

~ Life ~

Run Away

That screaming you heard
in the middle of the night
was your nightmares running

from your heart's bonfire.

RUN AWAY
alternative beat

That screaming you heard
in the middle of the night?

Simply

your nightmare running

from the heat of your heart.

~ Life ~

When The Power Goes Out

When the power goes out
the birds still fly and hunt for bugs
the sun still shines
the wind still blows
the squirrels still forage for lunch
the single people still long for love
the teenager still yearns for freedom
the government still demands taxes
for wars that rage in far away lands

When the power goes out
cash is still king
blood is still thicker than water
no one holds a masquerade ball

When the power goes out
your breathing sounds loud
your heart, that sweet child inside, speaks of play, speaks of silliness, speaks of joy

When the power goes out
the only things that don't work
are what others said you needed

I Was Thinking About My Life

I was thinking about my life
about the mistakes I made
about the choices I made
about the man I was
and the man who stares at the mirror
and the man I told myself I was
and the man I wanted to be

not the man my parents wanted me to be
not the boy that my high school sweetheart wanted me to be
not the man that Hollywood wanted me to be
not the man who led others to battle

I was afraid when I made some choices
I was drunk when I made other choices
I was blissfully happy when I made still other choices
we all make choices, saints and sinners
we all make mistakes
we all live life

if we remove the fear
If we remove the happiness
if we remove the parents and the Hollywood impressions
if we remove the shame and blame of concessions

if we make choices without all that
the targets become one and the arrow is loosed towards a path straight and narrow

~ Life ~

those mistakes in choices allows us to see beyond the illusion
to feel the beat of the choice that rings true, straight and narrow

Ho Hum

ho hum, another medical crisis
ho hum, another monetary crisis
ho hum, another natural disaster
ho hum, another armed conflict
ho hum, another woman goes missing
ho hum, another mass shooting
ho hum, another drug overdose
ho hum, another child goes hungry
ho hum, another child goes unloved
ho hum, another political promise broken
ho hum, another tax increase
ho hum, another day of choosing love over fear

~ Life ~

Eventually

Eventually, the rain stops
Eventually, the drunk at the end of the bar shuts up
Eventually, the meal is served
Eventually, the power mower stops
Eventually, the raindrop finds your neck

Eventually, the bathroom will be vacant
Eventually, laughter will erupt in the most unlikely of places
Eventually, a crappy moment will be a prelude to a majestic day
Eventually, true love's kiss awakens you from slumber
Eventually, winter returns to the land

Eventually, all of God's children will see the face of creation
Eventually, songs will be sung of deeds long ago
Eventually, mothers will tuck their children to bed
Eventually, hate won't be everywhere

Eventually

Happy

If I want to make my soul happy, I choose between the path that splits left or the path that splits right.

If I want to make my brain happy, I spend my time in the clouds, with nary a foot touching the ground.

If I want to make my imaginary friends happy, I fellowship with them.

If I want to make the fairies happy, I have tea and song in a forest glade.

If I want to make the dragons happy, I soar high above the clouds and play tag.

If I want to make the system happy, I play by the rules and get a haircut.

If I want to make my passed away loved ones happy, I listen to their stories of valour and heartbreak.

If I want to make my ex-lovers happy, I eat worms and die.

If I want to make the gurus happy, I pay to sit at their feet.

If I want to make myself happy, I talk to a tree.

~ Life ~

Raging

Hey you! Raging behind the computer screen! Indignant at the audacity of someone else's opinion. Hurt that your world view is in question.

Did the first keystroke in a retribution post feel better than the 2nd? Did the 20th key hit even harder at the heart of the idiot than the 5th?

Smash the keys!! Harder! HARDER!! Vent that vitriol inside. The other is obviously deserving it. Loser!

Deep breath in! Deep breath out!

Clear the mind! Soothe the heart!

Now tell me true, where did the energy go?

Throw Away

If the mug you drink coffee from is important, imagine what that ratty old underwear is doing for you.

~ Life ~

2022 A.D.

The year of putting a frozen pizza in the oven and 45 minutes later opening the oven door to perfectly baked peanut butter cookies.

Shalt

Them: "Thou shall not talk to your inner demons."

Me: "Maybe that is why they are at war with you."

~ Life ~

Game It Up!

One can play the game that was.

Or one can play the game that will be.

The Devil's Due

Some say the Devil's greatest feat is tricking humanity into thinking he is not real.

I say his greatest feat is imparting despair.

Prose

and farming implements
and cooking accoutrements,
oh my

Angel

So, I'm in dreamland again last night. It's a beautiful dream. I play the part of an administrative assistant at a large hospital and I am helping fellow staff members. Boring routine job stuff like "here is a stapler and the room you want is two doors down on the left." Then during my coffee break, I go for a bicycle ride in a large garden area. There is grass, pine trees, and off in the distance to my left, the ocean surf is crashing against the rough rocks of the coastline.

I come to a building. Perhaps it's a large house, perhaps it's some kind of office. It's mostly finished construction but there are a few areas that need to be finished off -- more plywood, more wiring, more ... finished. The main room is flooded with clean, clear water that is about waist deep. Something else to note when I report back to the boss.

I see a kitchen nook that is close to being finished and there is a tool there, on the counter top. I pick up the tool, but it doesn't feel right. There is a kind of static electricity that hurts my hands - it's been infected. I drop it and turn as if to leave this place. A few steps and WHAM! an energetic elastic is snapped at my waist, turning me and pulling me backwards.

My stomach drops into a pit. I smile, recognizing the feelings that are coming up. It's the night side. The shadow. The dark forces. They are here with me and they want to play a deadly game of winner takes all.

~ Prose ~

I can't see them but I feel them all around me. I'm in human form. A pitiful, easily broken blob of flesh and bone. A mouse to their cat. I can feel their glee in deciding how to carve me up and delight in arguing over who gets what piece of what to them is a sure thing.

In dreams past, I would have crumbled. I would have given into the paralyzing fear of what goes bump in the night.

But I am not in the dreams of the past.

I am here now.

I speak with a strong, clear voice "Do you want to fuck with an angel??" As I say the words, my pokey, hokey flesh morphs into a Being of Light, a Being of Love. My light is strong and I see them now -- bat-like forms as if so many hieroglyphs painted on the walls. The hunters, having realized the game has changed, cringe.

The dream ends as I turn to leave, unmolested.

A Pitchfork, A Blanket And A 6 Pack

I do some of my best thinking in the shower. Some folks sing, I think and send out gratitude for the wonderful life I have here on this little blue ball of a planet on the edge of nowhere, well off the beaten celestial track.

Today, as I was showering I was whining, er ... explaining to the Universe that it was very unfair to be dropped down here into this planet without a few tools for dealing with the pressure of human living. Life can be such a drag down here, ya know? A few little groovy things like telekinesis or unlimited money would certainly help with the drudgery of day to day living! A show of hands dear readers if you agree? Exactly!!

So after very respectfully and rationally explaining myself to this audience of none, I took a moment to relax into the warm shower spray. I said to the water "it's like being dropped off on a deserted tropical island with a few basic tools and NOTHING else!! Some preposterous tools like ... like ..." I got an image of a pitchfork in my mind. "Yeah, like a pitchfork on a deserted island!! and, uh ..." I then got an image of a blanket. "Yeah, like a blanket too. What the heck good is a blanket on a deserted isle?? Oh and now an image of a 6 pack of beer too!! Yeah, like that will last more than a day!!"

"It's exactly that Universe! A pitchfork, a blanket and a few beers. What the heck good will those do!?"

Completely satisfied that I had suitably impressed the assortment of jumbo sized shampoo bottles with my

~ Prose ~

impeccable and irrefutable logic, I relaxed again. I turned around to enjoy the warm water dancing off my now cold back.

My mind cleared and I enjoyed the moment of being king of my domain. My domain in this case being all 3' by 5' by 8' of the shower stall. Then I remembered how useful a pitchfork was when I was growing up on a farm. The obvious answer to it's usefulness speaks of moving loose plant matter around but there are some pointy bits at the business end of a pitchfork that could be used to gather food or perhaps fend off an animal that considered me a tasty morsel.

"Huh." I did a couple of stretches to ponder this and surveyed my domain, making sure the shampoo bottles were suitably standing sharply at attention during their royal inspection.

Yeah the second item, a blanket, would be good for those cool nights when the sun went down. Yep. Check! Perhaps made into a tent or used as shade from the blazing tropical sun. Yep. Check! It could also be used for carrying coconuts or wood. Cut into strips, it could be used as a bandage or even a tourniquet.

Huh. "Ok, ok Universe, a multipurpose tool and a way to regulate body temperature are actually, maybe, a couple of good things to have when stranded miles from civilization."

"But!!!" I exclaim as I spun around to face the shower head in my best impression of a sleazy TV show lawyer who is making a point, "That 6 pack of beer! Absolutely ridiculous. I would have it drunk in a day. Two days at most." I reach for my razor and start taking a day's worth of stubble off. Daydreaming and smug that I may have lost 2 of 3 points of contention but I have totally got this last point in the bag. Totally. "Power down the loudspeakers, fold the chairs and turn off the lights as you lock the door on your way out; this contest is over and the human won. W-O-N! Yeah baby!! Yeah!!!"

I took a stroke with the razor and nicked my face. "Dang, I'll have to … …" Wait a minute, alcohol is a disinfectant. In an extreme emergency, pasteurized beer could be used as a sterile solution to wash out a nasty wound. "No no no! I won this argument a long time ago you uncaring, silent as a tomb Universe! I am King and Emperor and Dictator for Life here in my shower stall domain!" I look sideways at the blooded twin blade razor to make sure it isn't hiding a smirk from it's king. Then it dawns on me. "Wait a minute, the empty bottles could be used as water bottles, carrying water from the stream a mile away to my camp at the beach."

"Huh." If I break a bottle in a certain way, the sharp glass could be used … could be used to cut food, or bark or even cut the blanket to make a tourniquet.

AAAAAARGGGGGH!!! I was winning and now my ace in the hole was snatched from my grasp too. Double AAAAAARGGGGGH!!!

I turn the shower off and step out to grab a tissue for my cut. It's not that bad now, and almost closed off. I look in the mirror and acknowledge that a pitchfork, a blanket and a 6 pack of beer would be very valuable flotsam on a deserted island. It just depends on how you look at your tools available at the moment.

~ Prose ~

... I Was Asked ...

I was asked this evening "you ok?"

I expect you would like some back story to this ... story. So my friend, allow me to set the stage.

Picture this: it's 8:05 pm on a summer's evening. The sun is just starting to set. I go out about this time every day to the local city park. My house doesn't have a lawn and this particular park is covered in lush, well manicured grass. You see, I get a walk in and then go lay on the lawn, luxuriating in the coolness of the grass after a hot desert day. To me, heaven by another name. Usually I have the park to myself.

This evening, there was an older couple walking their dog at one end of the field. I see Dog Dad bend over to pick up the 'doo. Perfect. I go further along the path and pick my spot. I lay down on my back. Sunset is about an hour away, so there is still some heat in the air. I discover the grass is slightly moist from that afternoon's all too brief rain shower. Feels great to massage the grass in my outstretched palms. The bird song, the gentle breeze, the tranquility all playfully lull me into an easy relaxation and I prepare to enjoy a meditative break.

A voice calls out "you ok?" It's the same dad from a few moments ago. There are only 2 other humans in the entire park he could be calling to and I know they are at the far end of the park. So I look up, give a strong wave and call back "yep!"

I lean back into the bed of green I am on. It takes a moment, then it dawns on me that is an excellent question to answer wholeheartedly for myself. So I run the line down in my head:

full stomach after a nice meal? check.
clothes on my back? check.
warm comfortable home to return to? check.
faith in humanity restored? check.

It occurred to me that I was being superficial so I went deeper:
personal energy field glistening? check.
connection with God Source strengthening? check.
had beneficial interactions with clients this week? check.
am I excited to get up tomorrow morning and do it all again? check.
is my future filled with hope, joy and curiosity? check.

Yeah, I would say I'm doing ok.

"So how are you? You ok?"

~ Prose ~

Snowing Here Late December 2021

So, it's snowing here this morning. Quite a bit for Vancouver, British Columbia, Canada.

Slept in yesterday morning, but now I'm the first up at 6 am. I guess it was to enjoy a walk around the neighbourhood with no one else's footprints in the fresh snow.

As I'm walking in the blowing snow (it was fluffy and dry!! :-) I am enjoying the moment and the twinkling lights on the houses when a wave of dark emotion comes over me. The hardships this year, the loneliness, the death, the despair and the nastiness of some peoples' reactions to … well … everything finally got to me I guess. I broke down for a moment, releasing the pent up tension. Then I just as suddenly started to tear up with joy and love and peace. My heart got warmer.

There are over 70 celebrations at this time of year and one of the big reasons there are so many is the hope and promise of renewal and rebirth that this time of year affords, as my hometown slowly sleeps through a mantle of white winter bliss. I felt the joy of promised renewal this year more than any other year past. I could name names, but if you are reading this it is fair to say you are on the list of people who have assisted me and many, many others to dig a little deeper into their heart spaces.

Thank you. And to the one who embodied all this 2000 years ago, gratitude for lighting the candle that was too long cold.

~ Prose ~

Goom-Bye 2021!

So I am at the grocery store. It's a zoo. Me and everyone else is trying to stock up a bit for the New Years Eve festivities tonight.

I go to the bakery department and see a nice looking loaf of bread -- "3 Corn" is the label. Ok. That intrigues me*. I look at the ingredients. No corn listed.

None.

I motion to the young bakery clerk and ask her what the dealio is with corn bread with no corn in it. She doesn't know. She offers to ask her manager. I say "Thank you. Please do. I am curious about this mystery."

She walks off and comes back to tell me her manager doesn't know either. I let her know that I like the other ingredients and will purchase the loaf even if I don't have a clue why it's labeled something it's not. I again thank her for her time.

Then I heard Betty White passed. A brilliant, talented, very funny entertainer who played the "dummy" in countless roles. That's how I remember her anyway. Perhaps she played it more straight in her earlier works? Couldn't tell you. Never really watched her earlier works. Knowing, I would tell you.

Managed to find a Chocolate Therapy Ben and Jerry's ice cream tub on sale for half regular price at the grocery store. It's delicious!!!

Mmmmmm, chocolate overload!! Y-E-A-H!

Ever notice how when things are on sale the size, the flavour, the colour, the whatevers you want never seem to be in stock? I wonder if there is a way to somehow turn that around, somehow say a few words and have items in stock at great prices, just for me. I'm not cool like that, so I don't know what is correct to say. Knowing, I would tell you. Also shopped for a permanent filter thingy for my brand new coffee maker. When I ordered the machine in mid-November, it was back ordered until Dec 15th, but then it shipped out the day of ordering. Between delays related to unprecedented regional flooding, the generally crappy weather, the washed out roads, the stress-filled holidays and everyone and their dog ordering online this year, I didn't get it until 13 days later on. Lucky 13 indeed!

The new machine is not like the old machine -- I have 3 filters for that one. I paid something like $10 for all three filters 10 years ago. Between using my own ground coffee and NOT paying for the factory packaged pods, I saved a good chunk of change over the years. Now this single gosh-darn filter is $20 and comes with extra bits to fit all the machines that were conceived and marketed and landfilled in the 10 years since I last bought a new machine. I pulled the filter out of the box and got it washed up. One of the useless-to-me bits smelled horribly of chemicals and felt slimy. "Garbage can that dwelleth under the sink, please take this bit off my hands!"

~ Prose ~

Wiping my hands in 5, or maybe 20, paper towels to clean them up after the slime moment, my hands finally came clean. I then had the joy of struggling to fit the new filter in the machine, then turned in my man-card to look for the instructions. Because, you know, the box mentioned looking at the instructions! Couldn't find them. Knowing where they were, I would tell you. I am a man, so I just decide to man-handle the plastic bits and mash them into the f*%& machine. Oh looky! Turns out, one more of the bits is actually useless-to-me as f@#* too! So I toss that in the now burgeoning garbage can that dwelleth under the sink. At least this useless bit doesn't stink or slime me up.

To recap, at this stage: no coffee in my cup and I've just tossed out $10 of plastic from the plastic contraption I bought at retail for $20. If I knew to call that progress, I would tell you.

Knowing, I would tell you.   And that my friends, on this last day of the year, is Earth year 2021 in a nutshell to me.

* 3 corn bread is an old-time way of saying in modern language '3 grain bread'

The Coat

I had a favourite Uncle when I was little. Uncle Herby.

The kind of Uncle that taught kids to play with their food at dinner and always seemed to have a spare chocolate bar in his pocket "for emergencies" -- it was almost like he knew that I rarely got such expensive treats at home. His was the beer I swiped and chugalugged at the large family gathering when I was 3 years old. Sometimes I think that was the reason we stopped having large family gatherings shortly thereafter.

Did I mention he was my favourite? He was the uncle that gave my older siblings their first cigarette pull when they were far too young. My Uncle smoked for years, but that isn't what killed him. Oh wait, I'm getting sidetracked down memory lane again. It's hard to see the screen with tears in my eyes. Sorry. Oh, yeah, smoking. Siblings. They were maybe 8, maybe 10 years old at the time in question. I learned about this long after the fact when I myself was an older teen. My brother said something one day about Uncle Herby giving him a cigarette once long ago, while my brother made a face like "it tasted like shit bro" to enliven his story. Mom smiled knowingly like moms do and said "That was why none of you smoked." He was the uncle that had stories and jokes and adventures to talk about. He did uncle things with me like hunt and fish. And a couple good talks. Real good talks.

Have I mentioned already he was my favourite? Fast forward to present day. I'm going through my closets, determined to not shuffle boxes from one house to another without at least a good try at downsizing. Then I find it.   The Coat.

The Coat that was Uncle Herby's. My father handed it to me a few days after my uncle's funeral saying "It's a good coat Morgan, hang on to it." I did keep it Dad, for over 30 years and a handful of moves. I never wore it, just shuffled it along. I'm looking at that damn coat taking up room in my closet and I just burst into tears. The love I still have for a man long gone, the great memories, the desire to downsize and my shame at not having thought of Uncle Herby in many years just wells up inside like a tidal wave and now my shirt is wet.   I didn't mean to get busy, I didn't mean to forget him. Somehow I did.   My love for him is not tied to a coat. The great memories I hold of a man are not tied to a coat. Yet here I am tearing up and stressing out over moving the damn coat one more time.

I'm ready for a new chapter of my life. This new chapter means I need to travel light. Real light. The old baggage and the old ways I have carted about for decades are not in my best interest. So here I am with tears in my eyes, saying goodbye like I should have done many, many years ago to the man and the memories.

Goodbye Coat.

Tears

Standing here in tears.

The box currently in front of me has a scribble of "memories" in thin felt marker on it's lid. Like one word could ever tell the whole story.

I jettisoned my high school annuals years ago, but kept some photos, some letters, some postcards, a few select knick knacks from my early years. Trinkets of a happy childhood. That's how I remember it anyway. In truth, it was what it was.

I rumage through the box and find a photo. A photo of my high school sweetheart as she was long ago. Before she married someone else and raised a family of her own. My plan was to lose our virginity together .. that turned out to be not so much. Not so much of anything in that relationship except friendship. Stop telling me what a great friend I was damn it! I wanted us to bone! Oh yeah, that's right, I didn't make a move, not the kind a teenage girl would have appreciated and understood anyway. So here I am looking at yellowing paper instead of deeply into her beautiful, blue, middle aged eyes.

I gently put her photo to one side and roughly grab a small handful of other photos. This time I am holding my college life condensed into 5 photos. I see way too much hair and a really poor fashion sense. And what the fuck was up with my dorky glasses? Yikes! Oh man, what was I thinking??

~ Prose ~

By now, I am little less sure of my remembered past, and a little unsteady on my feet, I pick up a piece of paper that was written at a retreat. My fellow participants shared with me what they most enjoyed about getting to know me in the short time we spent cloistered away that autumn weekend. I don't even remember their faces anymore, but their words remain -- "what a great guy I was!" said 10 different ways in 10 different writing styles.

I see 5 career choices that fizzled and faded.

I see photos of ancestors long dead and I plainly hear their words of encouragement and strength "Do what we could not. For the love of God, do what we could not. Live life. Make love. Enjoy the sunsets and remember us sometimes." But they are not there in the photos, they are not there in the box. They are in heaven and at peace.

Why aren't I at peace too? Why are the tears coming on stronger now? Was my life a train wreck of shallowness and faked happiness? Did wasting my younger years make me stronger for what was coming next as I got older?

What do I keep and what do I get rid of from this box? Can I stop the blame game and just appreciate the rustle of experience as chapters lived turn softly and gently and fall naturally into the bonfire of a life lived with purpose and dedication that feeds a warm and expansive heart?

Remember The Oven Mitt

Mulling the future.

Chewing on the past.

Avoiding the present.

Such is life in the slow lane. Yeah, renting a cabin out of town for a month or three. Nothing special and a lot like home actually -- crappy bed, way too close neighbours, and annoyingly bright street lighting that washes out the night sky stars.

But the feeling, the feeling that LIFE is somehow different courses through my body. New town, big trees, different ... energy. And yet the past comes in waves to haunt me and the spectre of the future is daunting to say the least. These walls are a different colour than I am used to, the provided cutlery is dull, the plumbing is temperamental and yet the air is somehow cleaner, more ... alive.

Counting my blessings on one hand and being lovingly corrected by a friend who is beautiful and even more authentic than I, the Great One, the not-so-late Mr. Morgan Silas as my own insecurities and jealousy rages after an intimate conversation with her. Just another emotional buffet to love, cherish and ultimately let go of. This implacable advisor reminded me with her impeccable wisdom that mistakes are blessings, if one chooses to learn from them.

Bitch.

~ Prose ~

She is right of course, except that she is wrong in not knowing how fucking pig headed I can be about NOT learning a god damn thing. For example, I burned my hand yesterday on the crappy oven, putting a crappy ready-made TV dinner in it. 50 years on this crappy planet and one would assume that my grown ass would know that crappy ovens are crappy hot when in crappy use. Nopers! Not me. Crap.

What chance do I have to learn a really big lesson -- like, say, how not to hurt people that I love?

Gotta go, this Pavlov dog's dinner bell just rang telling me that the TV dinner is ready and hot in the oven. Maybe I am ready to remember the oven mitt this time. Maybe I am not. Maybe I am ready to be gentle with myself. Maybe I am not.

Cloud Girl

There are those who live and float in the clouds. Up above high, life is light and there is much freedom of movement. Closer to the Sun, closer to the stars, closer to God and closer to family. One such is Cloud Girl.

There are those who have remained ... lower. They look at their shoes. They watch where they step. They hoard and rarely joyfully sing out loud.

When you look downwards you are 'down'. When you look upwards, you are 'up'. It is all well and good to watch where you step -- there are puddles and poop and trash to trip over on the ground. You can also look straight ahead and see the dangers ahead with your peripheral sight. You can see your destination and you can see the ground with the litter and poop. Some are happy with that.

When you look up, you can not see your steps. You will fall down much. Soon, you will notice that you are able to avoid the debris. You will fall down less. And you will be 'up' as you are not looking 'down'.

When you bounce a ball in your hand, it is 'here' then it is 'up'. When you dribble a ball, it is 'here' then it is 'down'. The ball that is 'up' falls gently and softly to your hand. The ball that is 'down' slaps the ground and comes back to 'here' in a most noisy way.

The airplane that flies is graceful and free! It is 'up'. The airplane that is low, it is 'down'. It may crash, it may wobble.

~ Prose ~

When a plane is low, humans can be anxious. When a plane is high, humans breathe a sigh of relief.   Those who are "up' can peer down to see those who are 'down' -- those who are 'down' rarely look up to see those that are 'up'.   Cloud girl likes being 'up' and she is not understanding why some choose to be 'down'.

Man At War

The heart is a part of all of us. As a masculine human, the little bastard gets no love from me. I like logic, I like planning, I like smashing things with my manly tools. Oh, do I ever like smashing!

My heart is soft and warm and fuzzy -- it doesn't plan. It feels and moves with a flow of love energy. GRRrrrrr!! I want to smash it with my manly tools!

But whenever I try to smash it, it does not break! It squishes. It burps. It deflects the hard blow of my hefty axe so my swing was in vain.

I want to strangle it!! I decide to do just that!! But as soon as I grip hard, it pops out of my enraged hands with a moist PLOP! PLOP! PLOP! sound as my heart goes from my manly grip to the muddy ground.

Foiled again!

Stomping my size 13 boot on it just makes it skitter off -- far off from where I am. Oh!! That does NOT feel good!

Not at all!

I breathe in. I breathe out. I move, unbalanced and shaky, towards it to scoop it up. I cradle it and cuddle it some as I turn around and walk slowly back to where its home is. The walk clears me; clears my rage. I sense a change, a moment of understanding. My heart is here, close by, unmolested for all my smashing, and my schemes of destruction. If I desire to demolish, if I want to be hard -- that is elsewhere. It is not here. In my heart space.

From where I stand in my heart space, I can see the human man who is me plot and scheme. I can see myself construct great visions that glorify my ego. I can see a leader without a rudder.

From inside my heart space, I sense the notion of a tide inside me. I feel the motion of a tear as it starts deep, deep inside, and works its way slowly, so very slowly, up a dry, unfamiliar tear duct. Softly, quietly, the salty moisture is expelled, and I see the human man have a moment of release, a moment of connection with his rudder, his true North.

I see a vision of a man out there, far from his heart, drop his sword, drop his axe. The man of vision is me in human form, and I look to my heart with now human eyes. I see a fire. It dances with life. It lights a path I had not walked before.

I set out on a journey.

Sludge Attack

As I come off an emotional rollercoaster of a weekend, I realize that somehow we are all struggling right now.

Yes, that is a trite, contrived, populist saying. But hear me out for a moment.

There is a beautiful moment of interaction* -- perhaps a smile, perhaps a laugh, perhaps a glancing touch, perhaps a look that intrigues. Then, a tentative step forward to move a burgeoning relationship to a new level that is met with "Oh no, sorry, I am working on my own fears right now and can't go there in love with you."... "Oh, I see. Never mind. I am not important anyway."

Tidal wave over tidal wave of fears and doubts come crashing in from the ethers and I realize the other is just me, loving me into seeing where the hurts of life never got recognized and moved off my heart.

For our interactions with each other are but a dance..... "This is my pain, can you see it Other" ... "Oh, it triggers me! Why haven't your angels healed that for you Other-Me?" ... "Oh wait, what is this fresh memory? A moment of tragedy when I was 5, or was it 15, or will it be when I turn 50? Eeek! Stay away for I am broken!"

Your pain has trapped you, but it can free the Other's pain by recognition.

~ Prose ~

Who is this 'You' you may ask? Morgan Silas, of course. The Other-in-love, of course. You too, dear reader. Even the person over there is included.

The mirror reflects ad nauseam.

I see the Other, and in doing so, I see myself much more clearly. Yes, the bruises. Yes the tears, but also the smiles, also the joys, also the highs of triumphant action that we experience in this cesspool -- this glorious sludge that is life on Earth in 2022.

There is a beauty in understanding the dance. There is a beauty in watching dancers. There is a beauty in dancing. May you always choose to dance, dear reader.

*bonus paragraph: The jackass in the car that zips ahead in the traffic jam, saving precious seconds off his journey. RAGE! Anger at the cheater!! "Why can't he just pull in behind me??!" And yet you, dear one, don't you enjoy getting ahead too? Have you never laughed at pulling ahead of someone else, perhaps at their expense? Money-wise? Emotion-wise? Career-wise?

No Mercy

My theme song I am humming today is "No Mercy" by country singer Ty Herndon.

In the song's music video Ty is referencing a man/woman romantic relationship that was on the mend and very hope-filled at a happy ending. Within this particular moment of writing, love without mercy is indeed the overarching vibe.

My lovely muse is, however, also referencing breaking out of heartache in more general terms. The heartache of looking at the shit show that life here on Earth can be in modern times.

So stop looking at life as it 'is' and bring in the outrageous love that is beating in YOUR heart. Fuck the heartache. I don't mean to bury away the pain. By all means, acknowledge it. But don't make it central to your being.

Make paradise your being. Make paradise the words you use. Greet everyone as a friend until proven otherwise.

Love is the most powerful force in the universe....so why are we, as a species, so focused on less?

~ Prose ~

Storm Front

At the moment of typing this, my neighbourhood is on the leading edge of a snowstorm front. Little snowflakes occasionally waft through the air, highlighted by the sunbeams that are also playing in my space today.

As I gather my things to head for a walk, I reach for my new winter jacket -- it's red and very wonderful to wear when the temperature dips to just below freezing like the weather is now. I have other jackets to wear but I don't yet give thanks for the blessings of that multitude. I reach for my warm gloves and head off on my walk.

The outside air is crisp, but I am warm enough for a short walk. I start to give thanks for the warm house I can return to, the friends who were, and the lovers who will be. I also reflect that I am hale and hearty enough to go for a long walk around the neighbourhood. I am blessed to say hello to passersby who are also walking this fine day. I still don't think to give thanks for the coats I have extra.

I set off.

The snowflakes come down like so many balloons at the circus tent. I count my blessings with each one -- gifts from heaven. This one a relationship, this one a car, that won a brother, that one a sister.

Am I solid in my human-ness? No, not solid enough to my liking. And then I realize these gifts, these blessings are all just masks, just personas of illusion. I could sell everything and start over, or I could springboard to a new reality -- by choosing it so.

The snowflakes stop as I re-cross the line, the line where they fall and the line where they don't, driven by the wind from the storm high above. Everything is a gift, and everything is a choice. Now I give thanks that I can write this to you.

~ Prose ~

To My Friends

To my friends who are protesting against something, thank you.

To my friends who are protesting for something, thank you.

To my friends who are posting their opinions on social media, thank you.

To my friends who are not posting their opinions on social media, thank you.

To my friends who know exactly how to get the world out of this mess, thank you.

To my friends who have no clue how to get the world out of this mess, thank you.

To my friends who are going to vote for their usual party in the next election, thank you.

To my friends who are going to vote for a party they never would have voted for before, thank you.

To my friends who no longer vote at all, thank you.

To my friends who read this far, thank you.

To my friends who didn't read this far, thank you, too.

To my friends who read the last page first, I see you.

The Series

The series continues with

Whispers of the Deep
Bittersweet Renewal in a Love Lost and a Love Found
Flotsam and Jetsam Series
Book 2

Meet Morgan

Morgan has had a vivid imagination since his earliest days of childhood, fuelled in part by reading and watching favourites such as Star Trek, Space:1999, Battlestar Galactica, and the Belgariad fantasy series, all provided wonderful opportunities to explore beyond the ordinary of rural living. Being the youngest of 5 siblings, he was delighted that older siblings had bought fantasy sci-fi books by the likes of Arthur C. Clarke and Isaac Asimov.

Recently, the opportunity to explore more of his burgeoning imagination has led him to write poetry and ponderings exploring adult-centric themes in love as well as a children's book. His books *Echoes of the Deep, Whispers of the Deep,* and *Sammy the Gnat Gets a New Raincoat* provide perspectives on love and life to different ages and stages.

While always interested in the subtle world around him, Morgan began exploring his own inner world. This led him first to meditation and many wonderful and exotic moments. In seeking answers to his deeply held inner knowings, he has learned to trust his intuition. He has certification in Usui Reiki, Violet Flame Reiki, Akashic Record reading, Channeling, and Mediumship.

He currently resides on Vancouver Island, Canada. When not crafting wordart, he loves exploring the beautiful Pacific Northwest.

A Note To The Reader

Those words are from the heart. And the heartbreak. And the shattering of a life that was not.

I wasn't really a storyteller before these events, not like this. Not some 250 pages spread over two volumes anyway.

I have more to my story, I have more to say. Love and connections, definitely! Life and prose on what are historical events, for sure!!

As you journey through the intricate phases of love poems within the pages of this book, I want to extend my deepest gratitude for accompanying me on this poetic odyssey.

From the euphoria of first encounters to the profound depths of heartache, we've traversed the spectrum of love's complexities together. Each verse and line is a testament to the shared human experience of love in all its magnificence and tumult.

But our journey doesn't end here. If you've found solace, inspiration, or even a mirrored reflection of your own heart within these poems, I invite you to continue this exploration with me beyond the confines of these pages.

Join me on Facebook and Instagram at @MorganThe Wordsmith, where we'll delve deeper into the nuances of love, life, and everything in between. Let's continue to seek inspiration, share our stories, and find beauty in the ordinary moments that define our existence.

Thank you for being a part of this journey. Together, let's embrace the enduring power of love and the resilience of the human spirit.

With heartfelt gratitude,
Morgan Silas Donnelly

www.ingramcontent.com/pod-product-compliance
Lightning Source LLC
Chambersburg PA
CBHW050611100526
44585CB00034B/1257